323.1

HEREWARD COLLEGE OF FURTHER EDUCATION
BRAMSTON CRESCENT
COVENTRY
CV4 9SW

This book is due for return on or before the last date shown below.

2 5 FEB 1998

5148

HEREWARD COLLEGE OF FURTHER EDUCATION
BRAMSTON CRESCENT
COVENTRY
CV4 9SW

MARTIN LUTHER KING

by Valerie Schloredt and Pam Brown

OTHER TITLES IN THE SERIES

Picture Credits

All pictures, including the cover, except those listed below, are © Flip Schulke or from the Schulke Archives, Florida. The Publishers gratefully acknowledge his permission to reproduce them.

BBC Hulton Picture Library: 4 (both); Black Star, New York: Charles Moore 30 (below), 45 (both); Rex Features: 8, 9; Val Wilmer: 6. Map drawn by Geoff Pleasance.

The Publishers have been unable to identify the owner of the picture of Gandhi on page 12; any information which would allow them to do so, would be much appreciated.

The Publishers thank Joan Daves for permission to reprint material Copyright © 1955, 1956, 1963 by Martin Luther King, Jr.; Copyright © 1968 by Estate of Martin Luther King, Jr. The Publishers also wish to express their gratitude to Flip Schulke, King's friend and photographer, for advice in preparing the text and for clarifying points in the story. Without his assistance, the task of preparing this book would have been much more difficult.

This edition has been abridged from the original edition published by Exley Publications Ltd
16 Chalk Hill, Watford, Herts WD1 4BN, Great Britain.

Published in Great Britain in 1989 by
Living & Learning (Cambridge) Ltd,
Duke Street, Wisbech, Cambs PE13 2AE, Great Britain.

British Library Cataloguing in Publication Data

Schloredt, Valerie with Pam Brown.
   Martin Luther King—(People who have helped the world).
   1. King, Martin Luther. – Juvenile literature.
   2. Afro-Americans – Biography – Juvenile literature.
   3. Baptists – Clergy – Biography – Juvenile literature.
   4. Clergy – United States – Biography –
      Juvenile literature.
   I. Title.
   II. Series.
   323.1'196'024   E.185.97.K5

ISBN 0-905-114-99-X

Series conceived and edited by Helen Exley.

Picture research: Diana Briscoe.
Research: Margaret Montgomery.
Editing: Pam Brown and Gail Jarrett.
Typeset by Brush Off Studios, St Albans, Herts.
Printed and bound in Hungary.

MARTIN LUTHER KING

America's great non-violent leader, who was murdered in the struggle for black rights

Valerie Schloredt and Pam Brown

LDA edition written by Beverley Birch

Above: This photograph of slaves in West Africa was taken in the 1890s. In the US slavery was abolished in the Proclamation of Emancipation in 1863, but it continued in many other parts of the world. Slaves were dragged from their villages and families – to be bought and sold.

Right: A black woman is sold as a slave in America. Martin's grandfather was a slave.

Slavery

For thousands of people from Europe, America in the 1800s was a land of hope and freedom where they had the chance of a better life. But for the black people of America it was a different story.

For three hundred years, millions of black Africans had been taken across the Atlantic Ocean. In America they were sold into slavery to work on white people's lands and in their homes. Slaves were bought and sold like animals. Husbands were separated from their wives, children from their parents. Slaves could not choose where they lived or what work they did. They had no freedom: they belonged to their owners who worked them much too hard. They were not given enough food. They were often beaten, sometimes to death.

From the beginning of the nineteenth century, some white people wanted to stop slavery. These people thought that it was wrong for one man to own another man. The northern states of America abolished slavery early in the nineteenth century – New Jersey was the last in 1804. But in the southern states slavery continued.

"... we have in common with all other men a natural right to our freedoms. ... But we were unjustly dragged by the cruel hand of power from our dearest friends and some of us stolen from the bosoms of our tender parents ... and from a ... pleasant and plentiful country and brought hither to be made slaves for life in a Christian land."
from "A Slave Petition for Freedom", 1774.

After 1863 black people in the US were "free" but they were still very poor because they had no land. The economic depression of the 1930s hit black people worst of all.

In 1861 eleven of the southern states separated from the states in the north. They formed the Confederacy. The Confederacy wanted slavery to continue but the northern states wanted slavery abolished. The American Civil War followed. After four years of fighting, the northern states won. Just before the end of the war, in 1863, slavery was abolished in the Proclamation of Emancipation.

After the Civil War America became rich. For many people life was comfortable. But although black people were no longer slaves, their lives were often terrible. They had no land. They could not afford good houses. They did jobs which no white people wanted to do.

The economic depression of the 1930s hit black people harder than white people. And so, almost a hundred years after the abolition of slavery, life for many black people was worse than it had been in 1865.

A lot of white people believed that they were better than black people. They believed that all black people were lazy and stupid. In the southern states all black men were called "boy". It did not matter that they were old men.

"Jim Crow"

Slavery had been abolished at the end of the Civil War, but the southern states still made laws which separated blacks and whites. These laws were called "Jim Crow" after a famous black song.

The separation of blacks and whites was called segregation. Segregation meant that black people could not eat in the same restaurants as white people. They could not drink in the same bars.

The Ku Klux Klan

After the Civil War some white people in the southern states started the Ku Klux Klan. The name is childish but the KKK was, and still is, a terrible organization.

The members of the Ku Klux Klan believe strongly that white people are

This photograph of members of the Ku Klux Klan was taken in the 1980s. Although the Ku Klux Klan has lost a lot of power in the last thirty years, it is still strong in some southern states.

better than all other races. They believe that black people are the lowest of the low. They do not want them to have any power in the US. They want total segregation of the races.

And so from the beginning they have tried to make black people afraid. They hold strange ceremonies in front of a burning cross. They wear white clothes with peculiar tall pointed hats. But worst of all, they take the law into their own hands. If a black man or woman does something which the KKK does not like, its members will kill them. From the beginning many members of the KKK were important people in their towns and villages. For example, many were policemen. They made sure that KKK members were not punished for their crimes. Since the 1950s there have been fewer killings in the southern states, but black people are still very frightened of the KKK, and in some places the KKK still has many members.

Opposite: The Ku Klux Klan still holds its strange ceremonies in front of a burning cross today to frighten black people. From 1900-30 members of the Ku Klux Klan killed hundreds of black people by hanging them in public or burning them alive.

8

In the years after 1865 many people tried to get justice and equality for black people in America. But by the 1950s there was still a long way to go. They needed a leader to help them.

Dr Martin Luther King became that leader in the 1950s and 1960s. He led the black people of America in a great non-violent protest which changed the attitudes of millions of people in the US and all over the world.

Martin Luther King's childhood

This was Martin's home in Auburn Avenue, Atlanta, Georgia, when he was a child. The family had a comfortable life because Martin's father was a banker.

Martin Luther King, Junior, was born on 15 January, 1929, in Atlanta, Georgia, in the South of the US. He was named after his father. He had a brother and a sister. Their grandmother also lived with the family. Their home was in Auburn Avenue, Atlanta. Martin's father was a banker and the family had a comfortable life. "Daddy King", as he was called, was also a minister at the Ebenezer Baptist Church in Atlanta. He was an important person in the black community in Atlanta.

Although Martin's life in Atlanta was comfortable, he met racism every day. He could not use certain public toilets because they were for white people only. If he wanted to buy an ice cream, he had to go to a window at the side of the shop. If he went to the cinema, he had to sit upstairs at the back. He could not go to school with white children. He could not use the same libraries or parks as white people. He met racism in hundreds of ways every day of his life.

When he was very young he had two friends who were white. One day their mother suddenly sent Martin home. She told him not to come to her house again. She said her boys were too old to play with a black child. Martin was very sad. His parents tried to explain that white people were not better than he was. They told him he was as good as any child, black or white. But Martin was deeply hurt.

The worst time was when Martin was fifteen. He was in his last year at High School. He and his teacher went to a school near Atlanta where Martin made a speech about the rights of black people in America. He won a prize. They were both very happy, but on the way back to Atlanta something happened. Their bus was very crowded. At first Martin and his teacher had seats. But at that time in the South black people had to stand at the back of the bus if white people wanted the seats at the front. Two white people got on the bus after Martin and his teacher, and the bus driver made them stand up. Martin was very angry but his teacher was afraid. In the end Martin stood up. He said later that it was one of the worst moments of his life.

This photograph of some members of the Ku Klux Klan was taken in the 1950s. They looked like ordinary people and some were even community leaders. Many children were brought up to believe that black people were inferior to white people.

Lessons from Daddy King

Although Martin's father was important in the black community, most white people thought of him as just another "nigger". But he was a proud man and he did not accept white people's insults. Martin remembered a time when a policeman stopped his father. "Let me see your driver's licence, boy," he said. Daddy King answered, "See that child there? That's a boy. I am a man." Martin was proud of his father that day.

"On the one hand, my mother taught me that I should feel a sense of somebodiness. On the other hand, I had to go out and face the system, which stared me in the face everyday, saying 'You are less than.' 'You are not equal to.' So there was a real tension within."

Martin Luther King, Jr.

Martin's father hated racism and the laws of segregation. He once said, "I don't care how long I have to live with the system. I am never going to accept it. I'll fight it until I die." Martin Luther King, Junior, did not forget his father's words.

Mahatma Gandhi, the man who led India to independence from Great Britain in the 1940s. Martin wanted black Americans to follow Gandhi's ideas about non-violent protest. He believed that if they did, they could get equal rights with white people.

College days

Martin went to college when he was fifteen. That was three years earlier than most students in the US. He went to Morehouse College in Atlanta, which is one of the best black colleges in America. Martin knew that he was lucky. Very few black students got the chance to go to college at that time.

Martin's father wanted his son to become a minister. At first Martin thought differently. He wanted to help the black community and he thought he should become a doctor or a lawyer.

The President of Morehouse College at that time was Dr Benjamin Mays. He believed that the church could do a lot to help the black people of America. After he had listened to Dr Mays, Martin decided to become a minister after all.

Just before he was ordained as a Baptist Minister in 1948, Martin preached his first sermon at his father's church in Atlanta. He was only nineteen years old, but he preached well. The people who heard him knew straight away that Martin Luther King was a good preacher. Soon after he was ordained as a minister he became the Assistant Minister at his father's church.

The Ebenezer Baptist Church in Atlanta, Georgia. This was Martin's father's church. In 1948, when he was only nineteen, Martin preached his first sermon here. Soon afterwards he was ordained as a Baptist minister. He was Assistant Minister at the church from 1948-1954. Later, in 1959, he went back to Atlanta and was Co-minister of the church with his father until his death.

13

Crozer Theological Seminary in Chester, Pennsylvania, where Martin studied theology from 1948-1951. He was one of only six black students at the college. Life was difficult for him at the beginning, but he did well and came top of his last year.

In the summer of 1949 Martin got his first degree from Morehouse College. But he had not finished studying yet. In the autumn he went to Crozer Theological Seminary in Chester, Pennsylvania. Life there was difficult for him at first. There were only six black students at the college. But Martin worked hard and did well. He studied the works of great theologians (people who wrote about religions) and philosophers (people who wrote about the meaning of life). He liked the ideas of the American philosopher Henry Thoreau. Thoreau hated slavery and worked hard to abolish it. In the 1840s he was sent to jail. He said he would not pay his taxes until the government stopped slavery.

Martin also liked the ideas of Mahatma Gandhi, an Indian man. He had led the people of India in their fight to rule their own country. For many years India had been ruled by the British. Gandhi believed in non-violent protest at all times. He had led the Indian people in protests against the British again and again. He had told his people that they must be ready to go to jail. They must be ready to die for independence but they must never kill for it. Martin began to believe that black people in the US should follow Gandhi's ideas.

Martin meets Coretta

In 1951 Martin was top of his last year at Crozer Theological Seminary. After that, he went to study at Boston University in Massachussetts.

It was in Boston that Martin met Coretta Scott. Like Martin, she came from the South, from Alabama, where she had grown up on a farm. On 18 June, 1953 they were married by Martin's father at Coretta's home in Marion, Alabama.

Later that year they both finished their studies in Boston. Martin began to look for a job. He wanted to teach in a university but first he thought that he should work as a minister for a few years.

Back in the South

Martin got a job as the minister of Dexter Avenue Baptist Church in Montgomery,

Dexter Avenue Baptist Church, Montgomery, Alabama. Martin was minister here from September 1954 to November 1959.

15

Alabama. He and Coretta had talked for a long time before they decided to go back to the South. They did not want to go back to southern racism and segregation, but they both felt that they had to go back. They wanted to try to make things better for the black people of the South, and to be with their families who were still there.

And so in September 1954 Martin and Coretta went to live in Montgomery. They had a busy life together, although the church was not very big. It had been built just after the Civil War and about four hundred people went to it.

Martin got up at 5.30 each morning. He worked on his studies for three hours before breakfast. Then he went to do his day's work at his church. He was already a good preacher, but in Montgomery he became a *great* preacher. Every Sunday he brought together learning and feeling in his sermons. More and more people came to hear him preach.

In the spring of 1955 Martin finished writing up his studies. He went north to Boston to get his Ph.D., a special kind of degree. From then on he was known as "Dr King" or the "Reverend King".

In the November of that year Coretta and Martin's first child, Yolanda (Yoki), was born. Life in Montgomery went on happily for the King family, but times were changing.

The eleven states of the Confederacy are orange on this map. 11% of all the people in the US are black. In the past, most of them lived in the states of the Confederacy, but now almost half of America's black people (47%) live in the northern (green) states.

US-Canada Border

Special Places for Martin Luther King

US State Borders

Towns/Cities

Confederate/Union States Border in Civil War

The need for change

In 1954 the United States Supreme Court had said that segregation in schools must stop. Black children and white children had to go to the same schools. Many white people in the South were very angry about the Supreme Court's decision. By the autumn of 1955 nothing had changed in Montgomery. Black children and white children still went to separate schools.

Black people in the South were getting angry, too. They wanted the schools to

17

change. They also wanted to change the rules about voting. The law in the US said that black people could vote in elections if they were registered (that means if their names were on a special list). But in the South the whites stopped black people from registering. In Montgomery, for example, only 2,000 out of 38,000 black people were registered to vote.

Most black people were too frightened to ask for their rights. If they did, they would lose their jobs. And so they said nothing, but they were becoming more and more angry. The young Martin Luther King realized that better things would never come for black people if they continued to accept the system of segregation.

The back of the bus

Do you remember how, when Martin was fifteen, he and his teacher were made to stand up for a white man on their bus? Things had not changed.

On the buses in Montgomery the front seats were only for whites. Blacks had to sit or stand at the back. Black people could sit in the middle of the bus, but only if white people did not want those seats.

On the evening of Thursday, 1 December, 1955 a black woman called Rosa Parks got on a bus to go home. She worked in a big shop in the centre of

Montgomery. She'd had a hard day at work and she was tired. The bus was crowded. All the seats for blacks were taken so she sat down on a seat in the middle of the bus. At the next stop some white people got on. All except one of them found a seat at the front. There was one white man standing.

The rule was that if one white person sat in the middle seats, all the black people had to go to the back of the bus. There were four blacks in the middle of the bus that evening. The driver asked them to go to the back. "I need those seats," he said. Three of them went but Mrs Parks did not. "Why should one white man need four seats?" she thought. The driver asked her a second time. "Are you going to stand up?" he shouted. "I'll get a policeman if you don't get up." Again Mrs Parks said no.

The driver called a policeman. When the policeman arrived, he asked Mrs Parks, "Why didn't you stand up?" "I didn't think I should have to," she answered. Then she added, "Why do you push us?" "I don't know," the policeman answered. "But the law is the law and you're under arrest." Mrs Parks was arrested because she had broken the city's segregation laws.

Later Mrs Parks was asked if she had planned her protest. "No," she said. "I was just tired and my feet hurt." She was

Mrs Rosa Parks, the brave woman who said no when a bus driver asked her to give her seat to a white man. She was tired of insults and her feet hurt. The Montgomery bus boycott followed her arrest.

tired of the way white people insulted her.

Black people in Montgomery were very angry when they heard about Mrs Parks's arrest. Here at last was a cause which could unite everyone who hated racism and segregation.

The boycott plan

On the Friday after Mrs Parks's arrest, Martin and a number of other leaders of Montgomery's black community met together. Among them was Ralph Abernathy, one of Martin's closest friends, who was a minister in Montgomery too. And there was E.D. Nixon, a black man who had fought for black civil rights for many years. He had, in fact, paid Mrs Parks's bail. People had been angry about the unfair system on the buses for a long time. Some thought that all black people should stop using the buses, so that the bus company would lose a lot of money. Then perhaps they would have to change their minds. When people do something like this, it is called a "boycott". Now was the right time to organize a boycott.

During the weekend hundreds of leaflets were given out. The leaflets said: "Don't ride the buses to work, to town or to school on Monday 5 December. Come to a meeting at 7pm at Holt Street Baptist Church."

Martin preaching a sermon in Montgomery. During his time at Dexter Avenue Baptist Church Martin became a great preacher. Thousands of people came to hear his sermons. Martin felt that the church was very important in giving black people a feeling that they were real people. He felt religion should deal with poverty and injustice as well as people's souls. In church they were free of the white man and his unfair laws.

20

On the Sunday, the ministers of all the black churches told people about the boycott, too. The Montgomery Bus Boycott had begun. But how could black people get to work? Martin and the other black leaders spoke to all the black taxi companies in the city. They asked them to carry passengers for 10 cents. That was the usual bus fare. The taxi companies, which had 210 cars, agreed.

The first day

Martin got up early on the Monday morning. At six o'clock he was drinking his coffee in the kitchen when Coretta called him. "Come quick!" she shouted. They ran to the front window. The first bus was going past their house – and it was empty. The black people of Montgomery were not using the buses.

Later in the day, Martin drove round the city. He could not believe his eyes. All the buses were empty. The boycott was going better than he had hoped. Many people were walking. Some were using cars and giving others a lift. Some were even riding horses!

Usually about 17,500 black passengers used the buses each day. They were 75 per cent of the bus company's passengers. On that Monday no black passengers rode on the buses at all. The bus company lost a lot of money.

In the afternoon Martin, Ralph Abernathy, E.D. Nixon and the other black leaders met again. They decided to start a new organization, the Montgomery Improvement Association. To Martin's surprise, they elected him president, although he was only twenty-six, and he had lived in the city for just one year. His first job as president was to make a speech at the meeting that evening.

A black woman asks for a lift during the bus boycott in Montgomery. Black people who had cars helped others get to work. Many walked. The boycott continued for 382 days. During that time no black person used the buses in the city.

Dr King's speech

When Martin arrived at Holt Street Baptist Church, he found a crowd of

Opposite: Martin at home with Coretta and their four children. The picture on the wall is of Mahatma Gandhi, whose ideas of protest without violence Martin always tried to follow.

about 5,000 people. Inside the church was full and there were many people outside, too. There were a lot of television and newspaper reporters with cameras, too. The police were driving round outside: they were expecting trouble.

Martin was nervous when he stood up to speak, because he had not had time to plan what he would say. First he told them about Mrs Parks's arrest. The meeting immediately voted to continue the boycott. Then he talked about the things which black people had suffered because of segregation. Then he went on to say that they must unite in their fight against racism. He told them that they had right and justice on their side. "If we are wrong, the Supreme Court of this country is wrong. If we are wrong, justice is a lie," he said. The crowd was completely at one with Martin now. They were listening to every word. He told them about the dangers they would meet. He told them they must not meet violence with violence. Finally, he told them that above all they must not hate their white brothers. They must show love.

The crowd cheered as he sat down. The black people of the South had found their leader at last. Martin Luther King had given them courage, hope and unity. He would help them to find justice. That Monday night Martin Luther King

Martin was a great speaker. His speeches were powerful and persuaded thousands to support him in his struggle to win equal rights for blacks in America. He believed the way to do this was to break unfair laws and that the protester should bravely take any punishment that resulted.

showed the world that he was a great leader.

Three demands

Next Ralph Abernathy stood up. He read out the three demands of the Montgomery Improvement Association

1 Bus drivers should be polite to black people.

2 The bus company should hire black drivers.

3 The first passengers on the bus should have the seats, black passengers starting from the back, white passengers from the front.

Martin asked the crowd to stand if they agreed with these demands. The whole crowd stood up. The Civil Rights Movement in the US had begun.

The first rainy day

When the Mayor of Montgomery, W A Gayle, met Martin and the other black leaders, it was clear that he would not stop segregation on the buses. He said, "Come the first rainy day and all the niggers will be back on the buses!"

But he was wrong.

The police and the mayor soon stopped the 10 cent taxi system, but the

"He could speak better than any man I've ever heard in expressing to the people their problem and making them see clearly what the situation was and inspiring them to work at it."

Rufus Lewis, a Montgomery businessman.

27

Montgomery Improvement Association began a car pool. Over 300 people gave their cars with themselves as drivers. Soon the car pool was doing as much business as the bus company had done. Many black people still walked to work — they wanted people to see their protest.

The Montgomery Improvement Association hoped that the newspapers, radio and television would tell the world about their protest. And they did.

During the Civil Rights Movement many white people joined the blacks in their fight for justice and equality. Martin told black people again and again that they must not hate their white brothers. They must always show love.

The whites fight back

The racist white people in Montgomery became more and more angry about the newspaper and television reports of the boycott. The world was laughing at them.

The Mayor and the Police Chief, the two most powerful men in Montgomery, said they would be hard on the black protesters from now on.

The police often stopped the drivers of the car pool. They said they were breaking the law, even when they were not. Martin was stopped by the police and arrested. They took him to the city jail but a large crowd met to protest against his arrest. And soon he was let out on bail. This was only the first of Martin's many visits to jail.

Meeting hatred with love

Some white organizations, among them the Ku Klux Klan, took the law into their own hands. By January 1956 the King family were getting thirty to forty hate letters every day. The writers of these letters often said that they wanted to kill Martin and Coretta.

Four days after his first arrest, Martin was at a meeting. Coretta was at home with a friend. Yolanda was asleep in a bedroom at the back of the house. Suddenly they heard a loud noise. They ran to get Yolanda. At that moment a bomb exploded at the front of the house. It was amazing that no one was hurt.

Martin left his meeting as soon as he heard the terrible news. He arrived home to find a large crowd of angry black

"If we don't stop helping these African flesh eaters, we will soon wake up and find Reverend King in the White House."
from a leaflet sent by white segregationists.

A member of the terrible Ku Klux Klan. During the bus boycott Martin got a letter which said, "If you let niggers go back on the buses and sit in the front seats, we're going to burn down 50 houses including yours."

29

Above: White segregationists were working hard to stop blacks getting equal rights.

Below: A Ku Klux Klan sign "welcomes" visitors.

people outside the house. Many were carrying knives, stones or broken bottles. The Police Chief and the Mayor were there, too, but they could not control the crowd. Martin realized that the crowd was becoming dangerous. He immediately went out and spoke to them.

"My wife and daughter are all right," he said. "I want you all to go home ... We cannot solve this problem with violence. We must meet hatred with love. Remember," he went on, "if I am stopped, this movement will not stop, because God is with this movement."

The dangerous moment had passed. The crowd began to go home.

The boycott continues

All through the early months of 1956 the black community continued their boycott. They did not use the buses: they walked.

The Mayor and many of the whites in the city tried hard to break the boycott. They found an old Alabama law which said that boycotts were illegal. Under that law, Martin and eighty-eight other people were arrested. Martin was the first person ever to be found guilty under that law. He immediately appealed to a higher court. He had to wait many months for a result.

At the same time another case was being heard in the Federal Court. The

Above: White women shouting "Hate! Hate! Hate!" during a protest march in Montgomery.

Left: White segregationists stood on the pavements during the protest marches. They often carried signs which said, "Segregation for ever!" "Go home to Africa!" or, as here, "Keep Alabama white!"

31

Coretta King with her
youngest daughter,
Bunny.

Right: Coretta with
Bunny, Marty and Yoki.

Coretta and Martin march together. Coretta stood by Martin through all the years of danger. She kept their family close and loving although Martin was often away from home. Coretta said of her husband, "He was a good man – such a very good man." She says he was a truly humble man and never felt good enough to deserve his fame.

Montgomery Improvement Association wanted the court to say that bus segregation was illegal. In June the Federal Court said that it was, but the Mayor appealed to the Supreme Court.

In November 1956 the city said that the car pool was illegal. Was this the end of the boycott?

The Supreme Court decides

On 13 November Martin was in court in Montgomery. He was listening to the case against the car pool. He was worried and sad. Was this the end of all their hopes?

Suddenly a newspaper reporter gave him a piece of paper. It was a telegram

"There was never a moment when we were not united in our love and dedication, never a moment that I wanted to be anything but the wife of Martin Luther King."
Coretta Scott-King, from "My Life with Martin Luther King".

33

from Washington. The US Supreme Court agreed with the Federal Court — segregation on the buses in Alabama was illegal. The boycott was over. The Montgomery Improvement Association had won.

The buses did not change overnight. The black community had to wait a few weeks more. Martin knew that the white segregationists would not accept the court's decision quietly. He was right. The Ku Klux Klan marched through the streets. But this time the blacks did not run away. They stayed and watched. They had found new courage.

One night bombs exploded in four black churches and at the homes of two black ministers. Soon after that another bomb was thrown at the Kings' house, but luckily it did not explode.

When segregation on the buses finally ended on 21 December, 1956, Martin Luther King was the first black passenger. With him was Rosa Parks, the brave woman who had begun it all. The leaders of the black and the white communities who had fought so long for the end of segregation were with him, too.

As Martin got on the bus, the white driver said, "I believe you are the Reverend King, aren't you?" "Yes, I am," Martin answered. "We're glad to have you with us this morning," the driver added.

Civil Rights Movement grows

Montgomery was only the beginning. It gave courage and hope to black people all over the southern states of America. Protests and boycotts began in many places. But the black community had to be united. In January 1957 the Southern Christian Leadership Conference (SCLC) was started with Martin Luther King as its president.

Martin was now clearly the leader of the black Civil Rights Movement. His life became more and more busy. He was asked to speak at meetings all over the country, and he wanted to do as much as he could to help the movement. But he

"We are on the move now," said King in one speech. "... Like an idea whose time has come, not even the marching of mighty armies can stop us. We're moving to the land of freedom."
"Freedom" was the word which was on the lips of all protesters during the Civil Rights Movement.

35

Above: Martin with his younger son, Dexter Scott.

Right: Martin with his first son, Martin Luther King III (Marty).

"My husband often told the children that if a man had done nothing that was worth dying for, then he was not fit to live. He said also that it's not how long you live, but how well you live."
Coretta Scott-King, from "My Life with Martin Luther King".

never had enough time. In 1957 and 1958 he made 208 speeches. His time at home with Coretta, Yolanda and their new baby son was very short. But with Coretta's help, the family was loving and close.

Martin worked very, very hard, although he was often tired. He had to tell the world about the problems of black people in the South. It was a difficult time for him.

Above: Martin playing baseball with Marty. Left: A happy moment in the garden with Bunny, his youngest daughter. Although Martin was very busy going to meetings and making speeches, he would try his best to find a little time to play and laugh with his children.

On 10 September, 1958 Martin was in a bookshop in Harlem in New York. He was signing copies of his book for the customers. A middle-aged black woman came up to him. "Are you Martin Luther King?" she asked. "Yes, I am," he answered. Suddenly the woman took out a steel letter knife and pushed it into Martin's body. Martin was rushed to hospital. The knife was still in his body. It was lucky that Martin had stayed completely still when the knife was in his body. A doctor said later that if he had sneezed or coughed, he would have died.

The woman who had attacked him was mad. Her name was Isola Curry.

At the end of November 1959 Martin decided to leave Montgomery and move to Atlanta. Martin became Co-minister, with his father, of the Ebenezer Baptist Church. He needed more time for his work as the President of the SCLC.

The student movement

Segregation on the buses had been only one problem for black people in the South.

In 1960 a black student went into a restaurant at the bus station in Greensboro', North Carolina. The restaurant would not serve him. And so the student and two of his friends began their protest. They followed Martin's ideas of non-violence carefully. Day after day they went to the restaurant and sat down. More and more students joined them. They were never served. Newspapers began to report the story. Sit-ins began all over the South, in restaurants, shops, theatres, libraries — anywhere where black people were not served. The students started the Student Non-violent Coordinating Committee (SNCC) to help each other.

"The greatness of this period was that we armed ourselves with dignity and self-respect. The greatness of this period was that we straightened our backs up. And a man can't ride your back unless it's bent."
Martin Luther King, Jr.

Martin gave the SNCC a lot of help. He often joined them at their sit-ins. During one sit-in at Atlanta in June, 1960, he and seventy-five other people were arrested. All the seventy-five except Martin were set free after a few days.

When his case came to court, Martin was found guilty. He was given four months hard labour in the state jail. It was a very heavy sentence.

The next morning Coretta had a telephone call from John F Kennedy, who was the Democratic candidate in the US presidential election that autumn. He said that he had been shocked when he had heard about Martin's sentence. He wanted to help. Coretta thanked him. A few days later Martin was home again. Robert Kennedy, John's brother, had spoken to the judge of Martin's case. He had asked for bail. The judge had agreed.

The Freedom Riders

The sit-ins worked well. Many restaurants and big shops began to serve black people in the early 1960s. But there was still segregation in many other places.

In the summer of 1961 a new kind of protest was tried – the Freedom Ride to end segregation on the buses between states as well as the buses in cities and towns. They held sit-ins in bus stations.

"The nonviolent approach does not immediately change the heart of the oppressor. It first does something to the hearts and souls of those committed to it. It gives them new self-respect; it calls up resources of strength and courage that they did not know they had. Finally it reaches the opponent and so stirs his conscience that reconciliation becomes a reality."
Martin Luther King, Jr.

The first Freedom Riders' bus after it was attacked in Anniston, Alabama. A white gang smashed the bus, set it on fire and beat up the passengers. Nine white men were later caught, but they were not punished.

For ten days they did not meet any trouble. But the white segregationists in the South were very angry. When the first Freedom Riders reached Alabama, they were attacked with great violence by members of the Ku Klux Klan. The students did not fight back. A number of the students were almost killed and then the Klansmen set fire to their bus.

Martin was deeply shocked by the violence of the Klansmen. On the evening of 21 May he was speaking to a meeting at the First Baptist Church in Montgomery. He was asking people to help the Freedom Riders. A group of white segregationists was outside the church. First they set fire to some cars. Smoke filled the air. Then stones and gas bombs were thrown. Was this the end?

But the law still had some power. A

group of National Guard soldiers arrived in time. All the people inside the church were saved.

The end of Jim Crow

The violence that met the Freedom Riders grew during the summer of 1961. But newspaper and television reporters saw what happened, and they told the world about it. People everywhere were shocked. In the end the Freedom Riders won. The US Supreme Court decided that segregation on buses between states and at their bus stations was illegal.

But there was still a long way to go on the road to equal rights.

Martin and the other black civil rights leaders decided that they had to widen their protest. It was time to change the attitude of the whole country.

The SCLC decided that they had to fight racism in Alabama. They chose to start in Birmingham, one of the richest cities in the South. If they could end segregation in Birmingham, they could perhaps end it all over the US.

The protest sit-ins, boycotts and marches began in April 1963. The protesters wanted to end segregation and to make the city give black people equality with white people at work.

One of the leaders of the white segregationists was T Eugene Connor,

known as Bull Connor. He was the Commissioner of Public Safety in the city. He was a hard segregationist. He said that "blood would run in the streets of Birmingham" before he would agree to desegregation. To him all black people were "dirty niggers".

Letter from Birmingham Jail

During the first big protest march on 12 April, Martin and many others were arrested. Martin was taken to Birmingham Jail.

While Martin was in jail some white ministers wrote to the Birmingham newspaper. They said that Martin was an outsider. He had no right to come to Birmingham. They asked all black people in the city to stop their protest.

Martin was very hurt by the ministers' letter. But how could he answer them? He had no paper in jail – the police would not give him any. And so he used all the small pieces of paper he had – bags, toilet paper, the edges of newspapers – and he wrote down everything he believed. This became his *Letter from a Birmingham Jail*. It is one of the most important documents of the Civil Rights Movement in the US.

The white ministers had called Martin an outsider. He answered, "I am in Birmingham because injustice is here.

Opposite: Martin in jail in Birmingham, Alabama. He was arrested, along with nine hundred others, for marching and singing freedom songs. The jails were so full, they couldn't arrest everyone! For eight days he was alone. During that time he wrote his "Letter from a Birmingham Jail", one of the most important documents of the Civil Rights Movement.

Injustice is universal – it has nothing to do with insiders or outsiders." He explained that non-violent protests were necessary. They made people see that something was wrong. He could not agree that it was the wrong time for protests. As a black man, he said, "For years now I have heard the word 'Wait'. This 'wait' has always meant 'never'."

Letter from a Birmingham Jail soon appeared in newspapers, magazines and leaflets all over the US.

After eight days Martin was set free. President Kennedy had helped. He had asked Birmingham's Police Chief to let Martin see his lawyer. The protest marches continued. But the black community was losing heart. So many people had been arrested. And so Martin and the other black leaders decided to ask for help from the students. To their surprise school children wanted to join the protest, too. The leaders thought carefully about the dangers. But in the end they let the children join the protest marches.

On Thursday, 2 May, 1963, a thousand children joined the march through the city from the Sixteenth Baptist Church. "We want freedom!" they shouted. By the end of the day 800 people were in jail. Hundreds of children had been arrested. The police had to use school buses to take them to jail.

44

The next day more children and students marched through the city again. The police told them to stop, but they did not. "All right," Bull Connor shouted. "Let them have it!"

Then the Birmingham firemen turned on their hoses. Great jets of water hit the protesters. Children fell to the ground like pieces of paper. Many were badly hurt by the water. Some protesters began to fight with the police. Then the police let their dogs go. The dogs attacked the protesters. Bull Connor only laughed. "Look at those niggers run!" he shouted.

But all through the march the television cameras were working. The next· day

people all over the US saw the terrible pictures – the smiling policemen, the angry dogs, the frightened children. They were deeply shocked.

Victory for non-violent protest

And still the black community in Birmingham did not stop their protest. Every day they went out into the streets. Every day they met the violent police. Every day they sang their songs of freedom.

And then – on 5 May, 1963 – something wonderful happened.

Some black ministers were leading a protest march to Birmingham Jail when they met a line of policemen. The marchers went down on their knees and prayed for a few minutes. Then they stood up and walked forward.

Connor was there. "Turn on the hoses!" he shouted to his firemen. "Turn on the hoses!" But the police and the firemen did not move. They looked at the quiet faces of the marchers and then they moved back. They let the marchers go through.

Connor was very, very angry. He could do nothing.

Martin's belief in the goodness of all men was right. Non-violent protest had won a victory in Birmingham, but at great cost – 3,000 people had been arrested during the protests.

Bull Connor and Abe Lincoln

At last white businessmen in Birmingham agreed to give blacks equality with whites at work. The city started a special group to try to solve the problems between the black and the white communities. The protesters in jail were set free.

More important, the federal laws on civil rights were changed. President Kennedy put forward a new Civil Rights Bill to the US Congress. He said later that "Bull Connor has done as much for civil rights as Abraham Lincoln!"

Bull Connor had made the American people think for the first time about justice for the black community. He lost his job as Commissioner of Public Safety in Birmingham and lost the next election.

During the protest marches many young people put a sign of equality on their faces. They wanted to show that they believed in the cause of black civil rights.

The 1963 march on Washington

Later that summer, a big march was planned in Washington, DC. It took place on 28 August, 1963. A quarter of a million people walked down Pennsylvania Avenue to the Lincoln Memorial. When Martin and Coretta arrived their hearts stopped for a moment. They had hoped for 100,00 people – 250,000 was a dream come true! About half the marchers were black and half were white. It showed that more and more white people understood the blacks' problems.

47

The march along Pennsylvania Avenue to the Lincoln Memorial in Washington, DC on 28 August, 1963. 250,000 people joined the biggest protest march of the Civil Rights Movement. It was 100 years since the Proclamation of Emancipation had abolished slavery in the US. The marchers shouted, "We want the freedom in 1963 which was promised in 1863!"

It was exactly a hundred years since the Proclamation of Emancipation had abolished slavery during the Civil War. Many of the marchers carried signs which said, "Give us the freedom in 1963 which was promised in 1863!"

Martin stood for everything that the crowd believed in. He had planned his speech carefully. He wanted to find exactly the right words to change people's attitudes and their hearts.

When he began, he spoke of the equality which the Proclamation of Emancipation had promised a hundred years earlier. He said that black people still did not have that equality. The crowd cheered Martin – they agreed with him completely. Martin knew then that he spoke *for* the crowd as well as *to* them.

"I have a dream"

Moved by their support, he put away his notes and spoke from his heart. And from his heart came the greatest speech of the Civil Rights Movement in America. His speech that day has become part of history.

Martin on the steps of the Lincoln Memorial in Washington, DC. He made the greatest speech of his life on that day. His "I have a dream" speech has become part of American history.

He repeated again and again the words "I have a dream". Martin dreamt that one day America would put into practice the belief that all men are equal. He dreamt that one day the children of slaves and the children of slave owners would be friends. He dreamt that freedom and justice would at last come to all the states of America. He dreamt that all people would join hands and sing the words of the great black song, "Free at last! Free at last! Thank God Almighty, we are free at last!"

When he had finished the crowd cheered and cheered. He had given a voice to the Civil Rights Movement in America. The newspapers that day said that Martin had become the "President of black America". 28 August, 1963 had been a great day in Martin Luther King's life and in the history of America.

A hope too soon

When Martin spoke to the crowds in Washington that day, he and many other Americans hoped that the victory of Birmingham could happen all over the country. But that hope came too soon.

A few weeks later, on 15 September, a bomb exploded at the Sixteenth Street Baptist Church in Birmingham. Four young girls were killed and twenty-one people were badly hurt.

And then, only a month later, on 22 November, 1963, President Kennedy was assassinated in Dallas, Texas. He was shot while he and his wife were driving through the streets. The President who had done so much for the cause of civil rights was dead. Martin was very sad and worried. What would the future bring? Vice-President Lyndon B Johnson was doing the work of the President now. And he came from the deep South. What would he do for the Civil Rights Movement? In fact Johnson surprised Martin. Only five days after Kennedy's assassination he asked Congress to work on a new Civil Rights Bill. In the end the bill became law on 2 July, 1964. Vice-President Johnson, later President Johnson, did a lot for the black cause.

In October 1964 Martin went to Norway. There he was given the Nobel Peace Prize. It was a great moment in his life. At 35 he was the youngest man ever to get the prize. He gave the $50,000 prize money to the civil rights organizations in the US.

Selma, Alabama

Back home in America there were still great problems. One of the most difficult problems was that thousands of black people were still not registered to vote in elections. Martin and the other civil rights

"Few can explain the extraordinary King mystique. Yet he has an indescribable capacity for empathy that is the touchstone of leadership. By deed and by preachment, he has stirred in his people a Christian forbearance that nourishes hope and smothers injustice."
"Time Magazine," January 3, 1964, on naming King the Man of the Year for 1963.

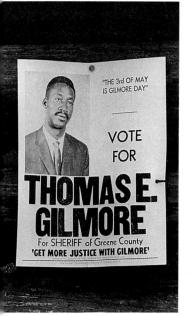

A black candidate standing for the first time in an election in Greene County, Alabama.

"THE 3rd OF MAY IS GILMORE DAY"

VOTE FOR

THOMAS E. GILMORE

For SHERIFF of Greene County
'GET MORE JUSTICE WITH GILMORE'

leaders decided that they must help. They chose to work in Selma, Alabama where only 150 out of 15,000 black people were registered to vote.

On 18 January, 1965 Martin led four hundred black people to register in Selma. They were told that the office was closed. They could not register.

On 1 February Martin and a large group of black people tried again to register in Selma. They were all arrested.

When he was set free, Martin decided the blacks must appeal to Governor Wallace in Montgomery. A march from Selma to Montgomery was planned for Sunday, 7 March. Five hundred people began the march from Selma but just outside the town the march was stopped by state policemen. The marchers were violently attacked. The police beat them. Fifty-seven people were badly hurt. For a long time the police did not let doctors help them.

Martin planned a second march for Tuesday, 9 March. This time he had help from many religious leaders all over America. But the march was stopped in the same place by one man from the Federal Court in Washington. He said that the Federal Court had banned the march. Again the marchers had to go back.

Soon afterwards three white ministers from Boston who had come to help the Civil Rights Movement in Selma were attacked by the Ku Klux Klan. One of

them was killed. All of America was shocked yet again by the violence of the white segregationists in the South.

On Monday, 15 March President Johnson spoke to Congress. He asked them to vote on a new Voting Rights Bill the next Wednesday. He realized that something must be done quickly to stop the violence in Selma.

On that Wednesday the ban on the march from Selma to Montgomery was lifted. The march finally took place on Sunday, 21 March. This time four thousand Federal troops guarded the marchers. The march took five days and by the end there were 30,000 people on the road.

Because of Selma the Voting Rights Bill of 1966 became law. At last black

An old black woman votes in an election for the first time. On 2 July, 1964 the Civil Rights Bill became law. President Johnson went on television and said that all people who were equal before God should now be equal in elections, in classrooms, in factories, in hotels, in restaurants – in all public places.

people in the US could vote in elections. And the Federal Government had the power to make the states follow the law.

Up North

Life for black people away from the southern states was not perfect either. Many of the parts of the northern cities where black people lived were very bad. People were poor. Many had no jobs.

By the middle of the 1960s many black people believed that non-violence was

not the answer to their problems. The way of non-violent protest was too slow. They could not wait for ever. The Black Power Movement, started by leaders like Stokely Carmichael, grew quickly. Carmichael believed that black people "must get power at any cost". There were terrible riots in cities all over the country from Los Angeles to Chicago to Boston.

Martin did not agree with the Black Power Movement. He continued to put forward his ideas of non-violence all over the US.

Stokely Carmichael, a close friend of Martin's, was one of many blacks in the middle of the 1960s who did not agree with Martin's ideas about non-violent protest. He was the first person to use the words "Black Power".

The Promised Land

In April 1968 he went to Memphis, Tennessee. The city's black dustmen were paid less than the white dustmen. The black dustmen wanted equal pay and equal rights with the whites.

On 3 April Martin's plane from Atlanta was delayed. Someone had told the airline that there was a bomb on the plane. There was not a bomb, but Martin was very late for his meeting in Memphis. He was tired and nervous when he arrived. He told those at the meeting what had happened. He talked about the dangers that he and his family had to live with.

"Like everybody," he said, "I want to live a long life. But I'm not worried about that now. I just want to do God's will. And He has let me go up to the mountain. And I've looked over and I've seen the Promised Land. I may not get there with you. But I want you to know tonight that we as a people will get to the Promised Land."

Did Martin know that he was near death? His speech sounded like a goodbye.

The next day Martin worked in his hotel room with his friends. They were planning the next steps in the Memphis protest.

In the early evening Martin and Ralph Abernathy went out on the balcony of

Martin's room. Suddenly there was the sound of a gunshot. Martin fell to the ground. He was very badly hurt. The bullet had exploded in his neck.

His friends rushed him to hospital, but an hour later he was dead.

This time the federal troops were guarding the protesters during a march through Memphis, Tennessee. The marchers were black dustmen who wanted equal pay and equal rights with white dustmen.

The death of non-violence?

Martin Luther King's death was a terrible shock to people all over the world. For many black Americans he had been their only hope. And now he had gone.

All his life he had tried to follow the way of non-violence, but after his death there was a great wave of riots all over the country. Thirty-nine people died and hundreds more were hurt.

REV. MARTIN LUTHER KING JR
1929 —— 1968
"FREE AT LAST. FREE AT LAST.
THANK GOD ALMIGHTY I'M FREE AT LAST."

Above: People all over the world were deeply shocked by Martin's death. On his gravestone were the words of the great black song which he had used in his speech in Washington on 28 August, 1963, "Free at last. Free at last. Thank God Almighty, I'm free at last."

"The day that Negro people ... are truly free, on the day when want is abolished, on the day wars are no more, on that day I know my husband will rest in ... peace."
Coretta Scott-King, from "My Life with Martin Luther King".

Free at last

The funeral service was held at the Ebenezer Baptist Church in Atlanta where Martin had preached his first sermon. His father took the service.

Hundreds of important and famous people were there as well as the world's television cameras. 120 million Americans watched the service on television and 100,000 gathered on the streets of Atlanta that day to mourn the death of their great leader.

Martin had not had a long life. He was only thirty-nine when he died. But his life had changed the lives of thousands of black Americans.

On his gravestone were the words of the great black song which he had used in his speech in Washington in 1963, "Free at last. Free at last. Thank God Almighty, I'm free at last."

Background information about black people in the United States

Slavery has been going on for a very long time. Slaves were common in Europe even as late as AD1200. In Central and South America millions of Americans were forced by the Spanish conquerors to work their lands and serve in their homes.

However, it was after Christopher Columbus "discovered" America in 1492 that large numbers of black people were brought over to America from Africa as slaves. They were used to the heat and they worked very hard. Their hard work on the big farms helped the farmers who owned them to become very rich. The first group of African slaves arrived in 1518. Between then and 1865 when slavery was abolished, it is thought that over fifteen million men, women and children were shipped across the Atlantic.

Most of the people who became slaves were caught by the kings who lived on the coasts of West Africa. The kings became very rich by exchanging goods for slaves.

Slaves were shipped across in very cruel ways. Mostly they were packed into tiny spaces to allow the captains to carry as many as possible. Each adult male was allowed a space six feet long by sixteen inches wide, an adult woman five feet ten inches by sixteen inches, a boy five feet by fourteen inches and a girl four feet six inches by one foot. Some kind captains allowed them out on deck while the holds were cleaned, but most left them in the tiny space for the whole journey. The journey could last up to three months. Many died on the way: 100 to 130 dead out of 150 were not unusual. One ship landed only 85 out of 390!

After 1713, Great Britain became the country to transport the most slaves. They shipped about 70,000 people every year to the West Indies and North America. The country made a great deal of money out of slavery.

In 1772 slavery was abolished in Great Britain. Lord Chief Justice Mansfield decided that "as soon as any slave sets foot on English ground, he becomes free."

The Founding Fathers of the United States refused to allow slaves to be imported in 1774. In 1783 the slave trade was stopped. They would have abolished slavery completely in America but two states — South Carolina and Georgia — would not allow it. They needed slaves to run their farms. In the North slavery was abolished early on. New Jersey was the last state to stop it in 1804.

From 1830 onwards, the North tried to get slavery abolished completely. As a result, in 1861 eleven southern states broke away from the United States. The American Civil War, between the North and South, followed. After four years of fighting, the North won. The Emancipation Proclamation was passed and now, at last, the slaves were free.

The southern states still carried on in their old ways. They refused to give black people equal rights. Black people owned no land and were not educated. They continued to live terrible lives.

In 1865 President Lincoln, who would have helped black people, was assassinated. The leaders in the South passed laws which stopped black people getting even the most basic civil rights. Because of their attitude, the US Constitution was changed in 1866 to give black people the right to be US citizens and to get equal protection under the law. In 1870 the Constitution was changed again to give voting rights to all US citizens regardless of race or colour.

However, the North more or less left the South to treat black people as they wished. The result was that, by 1895, nearly all blacks were not allowed to vote. Things became worse about 1900 when the Ku Klux Klan was formed again. Between 1889 and 1919 nearly 3,000 black men and women were killed by Klansmen.

In the 1950s, when Martin Luther King became the leader of the black Civil Rights Movement, most blacks were still poor and not properly educated. Although black people were allowed, by law, to vote it was very difficult for them to register in the South. Only five per cent had been able to register.

With King as their leader, things improved a lot for black people. But even today, twenty years after King's death, there is segregation between blacks and whites in some southern states. The law says there is equality, but white people ignore the law. The restaurants used to be open only to whites. When the law made this illegal, the restaurants simply closed. Government schools which were integrated now have only black pupils. The white children have been sent to private schools.

In some ways, things are better. Before the Voting Rights Act there were less than 200 black elected officials across the US. By 1970, there were 1469; by 1980 there were 4,912 and by 1986 there were over 6,500. This is only 1.3 per cent of the 490,000 officials in the US. There are 289 black mayors, twenty-eight of whom run cities of more than 50,000.

In 1959 55 per cent of black families were very poor. By 1987 it was 31 per cent. In 1989 the average black family earned only 55 per cent of money earned by the average white family. Many black people in the large cities in the US, such as Detroit, Buffalo, Chicago and Cleveland are without jobs.

However, many black people have been successful. In 1987 Bill Cosby was the highest paid entertainer in the world. Jesse Jackson nearly stood on behalf of the Democratic Party for the US presidential election. Pop stars like Michael Jackson and Tina Turner hold popular concerts across the world. Some black people run some of America's largest companies.

Finally, there are the thousands of ordinary black American people who have become doctors, lawyers, bankers and managers. It is thought that by the year 2000, one out of every three Americans will be non-white. As more and more become educated, it is possible that Martin Luther King's dream could come true before another twenty years have passed.

61

Glossary

Abolish: To stop something by law.

Appeal: When a court of law has made a decision on a case and has found a person guilty, that person often appeals to a higher court. He or she wants the higher court to change the first court's decision.

Arrest: When the police take and hold a person who they think has broken the law.

Assassinate: To kill a famous person.

Bail: The money which a person who has been arrested has to pay before he can leave jail. He has to promise to appear in court at a later date. If he does not appear in court on that date, the bail money is lost.

Ban: To say that something must not take place.

Bill: Congress talks about and votes on a bill before it becomes law.

Boycott: When a group of people say that they will not use or buy something.

Candidate: A person who wants to be elected for office, eg, in Congress.

Car pool: When people who own cars give lifts to other people who do not have cars.

Civil disobedience: When a person decides to break the law because he thinks that law is wrong or because he wants other people to notice that something is wrong. That person accepts that he may be punished.

Civil rights: A person's rights to freedom and equality with all the other people in his country.

Congress: A group of elected men and women who make the laws in the US.

Court: The place where cases of law are held, often in front of a judge.

Desegregate: To abolish segregation of black and white people.

Elect: To choose by voting.

Federal: In the US, belonging to the central government of all the states of America, not just to one state.

Government: The system which controls a country or state.

Governor: In the US the man who controls a state.

Guilty: When a court of law decides that a person has done something wrong, the court finds that person guilty.

Hard labour: Work done by criminals as a punishment.

Illegal: Against the law of a country or state.

Injustice: The opposite of justice – see below.

Jail: The American word for prison.

Judge: The top person who hears and decides on cases in a court of law.

Justice: When everything is right and fair there is justice.

Mayor: The top man in a city or town.

Minister: The priest of a church.

Nigger: A very impolite word for a black person.

Ordain: When a person becomes a priest or a minister he is ordained.

Preach: To give a speech about religion, usually in a church.

Protest: To speak out strongly against something.

Punish: To make someone suffer because he has done something wrong.

Racism: A belief that one race or group of people is better than another. In this book it means that white people believe that they are better than black people.

Register: To put your name on a list.

Riot: When a crowd of people behave violently and break the law.

Segregation: When one group of people is kept separate from another group. In this book, when black people are kept separate from whites.

Sentence: After a person has been found guilty in a court of law the judge gives that person a punishment or sentence.

Sermon: A speech about religion, usually in a church.

Sit-in: When people protest by taking over a building, or part of a building.

Slave: A person who belongs to another person.

Slavery: The system of people being slaves.

Supreme Court: The highest court in the US.

Vote: To choose someone or something by marking a piece of paper.

Important dates

1929   15 January: Martin Luther King, Junior, was born in Atlanta, Georgia.

1948   Martin was ordained as a Baptist Minister.
        He went to Crozer Theological Seminary, Chester, Pennsylvania.

1953   Martin married Coretta Scott in Marion, Alabama.

1954   Martin became minister of Dexter Avenue Baptist Church, Montgomery.

1955   Martin got his Ph.D. in Theology from Boston University.
        1 December: Mrs Rosa Parks was arrested.
        5 December: The Montgomery Bus Boycott began.

1956   21 February: Martin was jailed for the first time.
        4 June: The Federal Court decided that segregation on the buses in
        Montgomery was illegal.
        13 November: The Supreme Court agreed with the Federal Court's
        decision.
        21 December: Buses in Montgomery were desegregated for the first time.

1960   The first sit-in protest was held at a restaurant in Greensboro', North
        Carolina.
        The Student Non-violent Co-ordinating Committee (SNCC) was started.
        Martin was jailed after a sit-in in Atlanta.

1961   The first Freedom Riders from the North tried to stop segregation on buses
        between states. In Anniston, Alabama they were attacked and their bus
        was burned.

1963   Martin wrote his *Letter from a Birmingham Jail* after his arrest during the
        protests in that city.
        Bull Connor, the Birmingham Police Chief, ordered his men to use fire
        hoses and police dogs against the marchers.
        28 August: The first big protest march was held in Washington, DC. Martin
        made his "I have a dream" speech on the steps of the Lincoln Memorial.

1965   7 March: People on a march from Selma to Montgomery, Alabama, were
        violently attacked by the state police.

1966   23 people were killed and 725 were badly hurt during riots in Newark,
        New Jersey.
        43 people were killed and 324 were badly hurt during the worst riots of
        the century in Detroit, Michigan.

1968   3 April: Martin made his speech about the "Promised Land" in Memphis,
        Tennessee.
        4 April: Martin was assassinated by a gunman on the balcony of his hotel
        room in Memphis, Tennessee.

Index